FEW WORDS FOR STUDENTS

All thanks are due for the almighty Allah whose blessings helped me a lot to prepare the study material for the students of NEET. This study material series has been designed and prepared in such a way that it acts as a joint book for NEET and the students of 11th & 12th classes

From a long time a need was felt to prepare the study material for the intermediate students of classes 11th & 12th especially a joint study material for the students of classes 11th 12th and NEET. This was the urgent need so that students can prepare well for the NEET from very beginning.

Although a lot of study materials are available for the students, but there was a need for a study material to inculcate the concepts and ideas from text books prescribed by NCERT. So care has been taken to give a due weightage to the concepts and themes of text books so that students may perform well in future competitive exams like NEET besides this book equally benefits the students in their preparatory classes of NEET.

The bold or underlined words except headings or sub-headings are important points to remember for NEET entrance exam. Almost all the previous year questions of NEET come from such bold headings. Diagrams have been taken from diverse and authentic sources to make the process of understanding easier. Care has been taken to avoid the unimportant and unnecessary points in order to make the notes brief and easy to memorize, at the same time a great care has been taken not to avoid the important and necessary points. Long questions have been fragmented so that each and every concept is properly understood and at the same time a short note gets prepared for the sub-headings automatically.

Although due care has been taken to minimize the errors, but at the same time the appearance of errors in the study material cannot be ruled out. Therefore, i will be highly thankful for you if you write me about the errors which have crept in the study material. Don't forget to mention your name and topic where you spot an error. Will surely try to rectify the same in the coming editions, In sha Allah.

In the end my special best wishes are for all the students for their bright and shining future. Wish you always an Excellency in every field.

Irshad Aziz Bhat

M.Sc, M. Phil (Botany), B.Ed.

Morphology of flowering plants:

Introduction:

- Flowering plants also referred as angiosperms are a huge group of vascular plants in the plant kingdom. These plants show a great variety of form, shape and size. The size ranges from the *Lemna* and minute *Wolffia* (0.1cm) to the large-sized Banyan and tall Eucalyptus (up to 100 metres).
- Morphology of Flowering plants, explains the complete features of flowering plants, its structure, functions, classifications, significances and other morphological features of roots, stem, leaves, flower, fruits and the seeds.
- Plant morphology is therefore defined as a branch of botany which deals with the study of external features of different plant organs.
- The term, morphology of flowering plants mainly refers to the study of morphological characteristics and relative positions of different parts of flowering plants. The two main external parts of a plant include:
- **Root system**
- **Shoot system.**

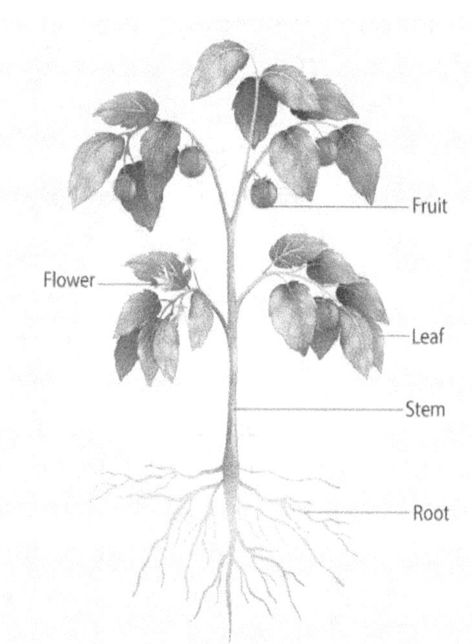

<u>The Root system:</u>

- The root system is the underground part of the plant developed from the seed embryo. It is mainly involved in anchoring plants below the soil, provides support, stores food and nutrients, absorbs water and other essential nutrients required for the growth and development

<u>The shoot system:</u>

- The shoot system is the aerial part of the plant, which is found above the root and ground level. The shoot system includes the stem, leaves, bud, flower, fruits and the seeds. Shoot system is one of the important systems of a plant.

Morphology of Root

- The root is an **underground non-green, descending** part of a plant, which bear endogenous lateral branches, a protective **root cap at the tip** and is devoid of nodes, leaves and buds. It usually develops from the **radicle.**
- Roots are the important underground part of all vascular plants. This part of the plant is mainly responsible for anchoring it down into the ground and absorbing the essential mineral elements, nutrients, and water from the soil. It is also used to store food.
- However, not all plants have their roots underground; some plants have their roots growing above the ground. These are called **aerial roots.** Like underground roots, these aerial roots are also responsible for absorbing nutrients, anchoring and affixing the plant by supporting them to the structures such as nearby walls, rocks, trellises, etc.
- Few examples of plants with the aerial roots are: Bonsai, Banyan Tree, Mangroves, etc.

General Characteristics of Roots:

- Roots are found in all the members of **Phanerogams.** It is important basic organ of the plants because of two important functions – **absorption and fixation.**
- They form the descending organ of the plant axis, normally growing away from light. Grow towards gravity (**Positively geotropic**) except for breathing roots.
- Normally roots lack chlorophyll and hence are **non-green.** However, roots of certain plants, which are exposed to light for long periods, turn green.
- Roots do not bear buds, leaves and flowers. They **lack nodes and internodes.**
- Root hairs are always unicellular.
- The root apex is protected by **root cap.**
- The branch roots are produced **endogenously from Pericycle.**
- Roots are generally sub-cylindrical, **tapering towards the tip.**

Functions of Roots:

- Roots perform various functions that are necessary for the survival of the plants. They are an integral or integrated system that helps the plant.

- **Anchoring:** Roots are the reason plants remain attached to the ground. They support the plant body, ensuring that it stands erect.
- **Absorption:** Primary function of roots is to absorb water and dissolved minerals from the soil. This is crucial as it helps in the process of photosynthesis.
- **Translocation of organic nutrients:** Sugar produced in the leaves by photosynthesis, is transported downwards to the tissue of the root where it is metabolised.
- **Storage:** Plants prepare food and store in the form of starch in the leaves, shoots and roots. Prominent examples include carrots, radish, beetroot, etc.
- **Reproduction:** Even though roots are not the reproductive part of plants, they are vegetative parts. In some plants, roots are a means of reproduction. For instance, new plants arise from creeping horizontal stems called runners (stolons) in jasmine, grass, etc. This type of reproduction is called vegetative propagation.
- **Ecological Function:** They check soil erosion; provide sustenance and also habitat to various organisms.

- **Food Storage:** It occurs by fleshy roots, e.g., Carrot, Turnip.
- **Additional Mechanical Support:** In some plants roots are modified to provide addition mechanical support. E.g., prop roots in Banyan tree, Stilt roots in Maize.
- **Haustorial Roots:** Roots of some parasite plants act as haustoria e.g. *Cuscuta*. They penetrate up to phloem of host and absorb nourishment.
- **Assimilation:** Roots of some plants are photosynthetic. E.g., *Trapa*, *Tinospora*.
- **Aeration:** Roots of some plants help in exchange of gases e.g. *Rhizophora*.
- **Symbiotic Nitrogen Fixation:** Roots of leguminous plants have nodules containing nitrogen fixing bacteria.
- **Floating and Balancing:** Roots of some aquatic plants store air and help in floating and balancing. E.g. *Pistia*.
- **Hygroscopic Roots:** Aerial roots absorb moisture from the air e.g. epiphytic plants, Orchids, young Prop roots of Banayan etc.
- **Climbing:** Some weak stemmed plants develop climbing roots which help the plant to climb up the support. E.g., Betal, Money plant.

Structure of the Roots:

- A typical root consists of following four regions. These merge into one another. The zones successively from apex to the base are follows:

Root cap:

- The apex of each root is covered by a cushion of thin walled cells known as root cap. In aquatic plants (e.g. *Pistia*) the root apex is enclosed within a sac-like structure called **root pocket**. Root cap protects root apex since it is the main growing part of the root.

Zone of Cell Division or Root apical meristem:

- It is just behind the root cap. It is the main growing region of the root where active cell division takes place. The region is about a few millimeters in length.

Zone of Elongation:

- It is about 1-10mm in length. This region is characterised by the rapid elongation of cells. The division occurs in relatively small number of cells. This region is responsible for growth in length of the root.

Zone of Maturation:

- It is usually one to several centimetres long. Here the cells, having fully expanded, mature into final form. Epidermal cells of this region give out root-hairs. These are main absorbing organs of root. Hence this, region is also called root-hair zone.

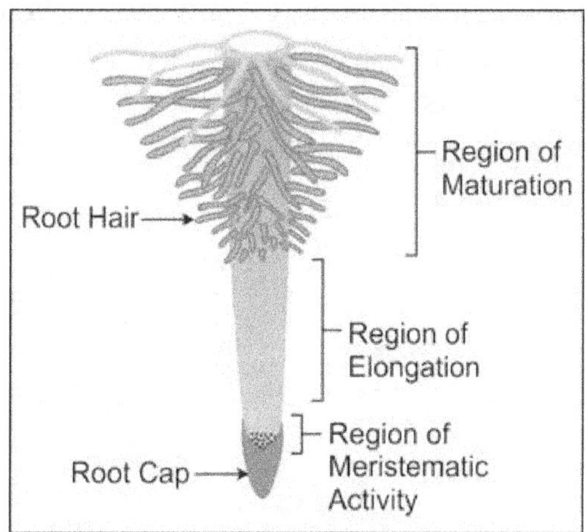

Figure: Structure of typical root.

- All roots have similar functions, however, their structure varies. Hence, based on these criteria, the root system is classified into two types:

I. Tap root system
II. Adventitious Root System

Tap Root System:

- The roots developing directly from the radical are known as **Primary root**. In most of the plants the primary root persists and becomes stronger to form tap root. Tap root usually produces lateral branches called **secondary roots**. Branches of secondary roots in turn are called **tertiary roots**. Taproots have a main central root upon which, small, lateral roots called **root hairs** are attached. Mustard, carrot, beetroot, parsley, China rose and all dicotyledons are examples of taproot system.

Adventitious Root System:

- Roots developing from any part of the plant, other than radical, are known as adventitious roots. On the basis of nature of development, the adventitious roots are further classified into three types.
- **Fibrous Roots:** In this type the primary root does not persist for long time and is replaced with slender, thread like roots originating from base of the stem. E.g., *Triticum vulgare, Oryza sativa, Allium Cepa.*
- **Foliar Roots:** Roots developing from the leaf are known as foliar roots. They originate either from Petiole e.g. rubber plant (*Pogostemon*).

Figure   Different types of roots : (a) Tap (b) Fibrous (c) Adventitious

- **True Adventitious Roots:** These roots develop from the nodes and internodes of the stem e.g. Prop root of Banyan (*Ficus*), roots from the stem cuttings.

Modifications of roots:

Modification of tap roots:

- Tap roots are modified into number of forms to carry out specific functions. The important ones are;

1. Fusiform Roots:

- The primary root is swollen in the middle and gradually tapers at both the ends. i.e., towards the apex and base *Rhapanus*, (reddish).

2. Napiform Roots:

- The primary root becomes almost spherical at the base and tapers abruptly at the lower end. E.g., *Brassica rapa*, (turnip).

3. Conical Roots:

- These roots are just like the cone, broad at the base and gradually taper towards the apex. e.g., *Daucas carota*, (Carrot).

4. Tuberous or Tubercular Root:

- These roots are fleshy and do not maintain any specific shape. *Manihot esculenta* (Cassava from which the starch food Tapioca is obtained).

5. Pneumatophores or Respiratory Roots:

- These develop in plants growing in saline waters. These roots grow vertically upwards. The air enters these roots through minute breathing pores called lenticels or Pneumathodes present on the tips of vertical roots. They are meant for exchange of gases. E.g., *Rhizophora*.

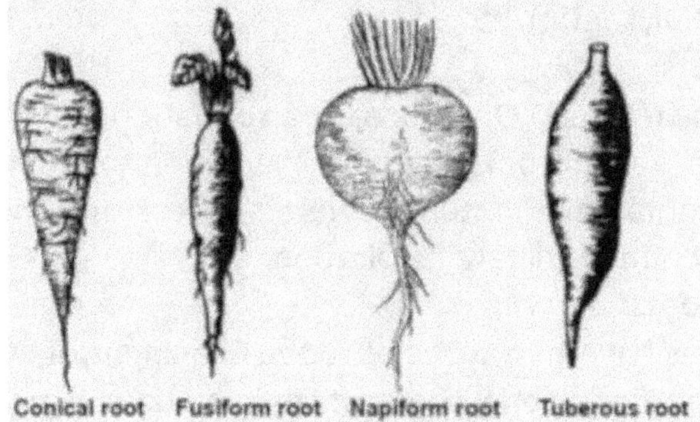

Modifications of Adventitious Roots:

1. Tuberous Roots:
- Adventitious roots that store food, become swollen and do not attain a definite shape. E.g., Sweet Potato, *Ipomoea batata*.

2. Fasiculated Roots:
- The swollen tuberous roots, when occur in clusters are called fasiculated roots e.g. *Dahlia, Asparagus*.

3. Moniliform or Beaded Roots:
- These roots are alternatively swollen and constricted and giving a beaded appearance e.g. *Dioscorea alata*.

4. Nodulose Roots:
- The adventitious roots swell only near their apices like single bead e.g. Mango-ginger, (*Curcurma Amanda*).

5. Annulated Roots:
- This type of root has many ring-like swellings placed at the top of other, Ipecac.

6. Prop Roots (Columnar Roots):
- In banyan tree (*Ficus benghalensis*) and Indian rubber plant *Ficus elastic* many adventitious roots arise from the horizontal branches of the stem and grow vertically downward. They become thick Pillar-like and provide mechanical support to giant trees.

7. Stilt Roots:
- These are small stout roots growing obliquely from the basal nodes of the main stem. They provide mechanical support e.g. *Zea mays*.

8. Climbing Roots:
- These roots arise from nodes and internodes of many climbers. They help the plant in fixing themselves to their support. E.g., *Pothos*, (money plant), *Piper betal*, (betal), etc.

9. Floating Roots:
- In *Jussiaea* (Family- Onagraceae), an aquatic plant, tufts of spongy, soft and light roots arise from the nodes in addition to ordinary adventitious roots. These roots have in numerable air spaces and thus help in maintaining buoyancy and facilitate respiration.

10. Epiphytic Roots:
- Epiphytes have two types of roots. Clinging roots which cling to the host for support and aerial roots which hang downwards. The latter are green in colour and have special outer covering called velamen. It helps in the absorption of moisture from air as the soil moisture is out of their reach e.g. *Vanda sp*.

11. **Assimilatory Roots:**
   - Aerial adventitious roots by some plants develop chlorophyll and become assimilatory in function i.e. synthesize food. E.g., *Trapa, Tinospora,* etc.
12. **Parasitic Roots or Sucking Roots:**
   - Parasite plants develop roots which penetrate into the tissue of the host plant to absorb nutrition. These roots function as **haustoria** e.g. Cuscuta.

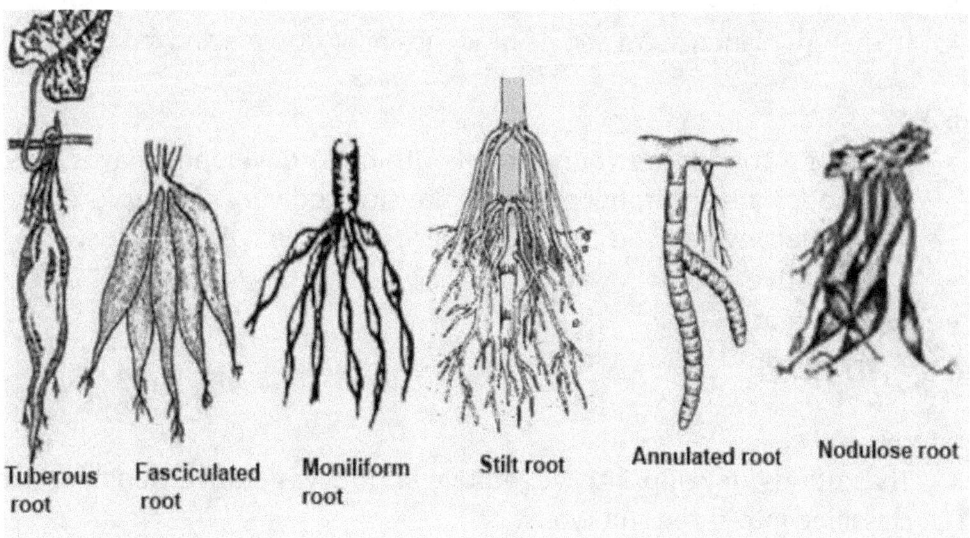

Morphology of Stem:

- The aerial part of the plant is called shoot system. It consists of stem, its branches and leaves. The shoot system develops from **plumule** (Tigellum).
- **Stem:** The stem is the ascending part of the axis bearing branches, leaves, flowers and fruits. It develops from the **plumule** of the embryo of a germinating seed. It bears **nodes and internodes.** The stem bears **buds,** which may be terminal or axillary.

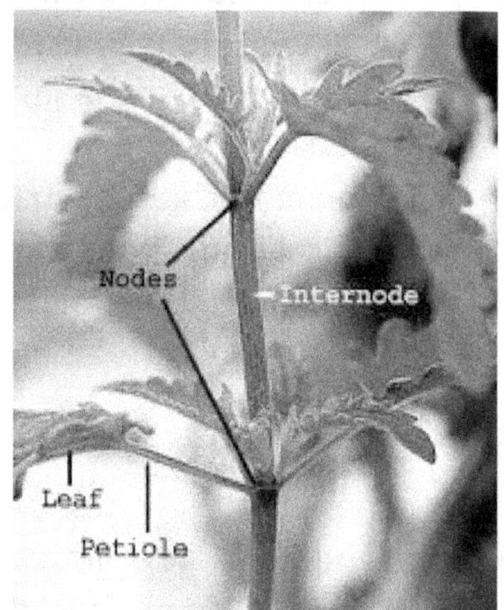

General Characteristics of Stem:

- The stem is an ascending axis of the plant and develops from the plumule and epicotyl of the embryo.
- It is generally erect and grows away from the soil towards the light. Therefore, it is **negatively geotropic and positively phototropic.**

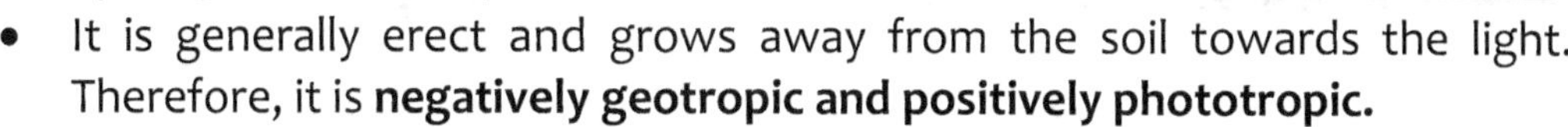

- Stem is differentiated into **node and internodes.** It bears leaves and branches at the node.
- The lateral organs of the stem (*i.e.,* leaves and branches) are **exogenous** in origin (i.e., from the cortical region).
- Shoot is usually green and photosynthetic.
- **Trichomes** (hairs) if present are either unicellular or multicellular.
- Stem apex is always apical.
- In mature plants, stem and its branches bear flowers and fruits.

<u>Bud:</u>

- A bud is a condensed young shoot with underdeveloped leaves. In a bud internodes are short; hence nodes are situated very close to one another and the leaves become crowded. There are three types of buds.
- **1. Vegetative.**
- **2. Floral and**
- **3. Modified.**

Vegetative Buds:

- These buds develop into vegetative shoot. Vegetative buds are further classified into three sub-types.
- **1. Normal Buds:** Such buds are present at the tip of the branches and the main axis and are called terminal or apical buds. They also occur in the axil of the leaves and are called axillary buds or lateral buds.
- **2. Accessory Buds:** Some plants produce extra some buds by the side of axillary buds. These are called accessory or supernumerary buds.
- **3. Adventitious Buds:** These are the buds which develop from any part of the plant other than those of normal and accessory buds. These could be listed as
- **Cauline Buds:** Buds that arise directly from stem e.g. rose.
- **Radical Buds:** Buds that develop from root e.g. sweet potato.
- **Foliar Buds:** Buds that develop on leaves e.g. *Bryophyllum.*

2. Floral Buds:

- These buds always develop into flowers. They are of two types:
- **Tendrils:** e.g. *Cardiospermum* (barren vine).
- **Bulbils:** e.g. specialised reproductive structures e.g., *Allium cepa* (Garlic).

3. Modified Buds:

- Vegetative and floral buds both may be modified for some specialised functions. These are
- **Tendrils** e.g. *Passiflora*, vine etc.
- **Thorns** e.g. *Citrus*.
- **Bulbils:** These specialised reproductive structures are found in *Dioscorea* (Yam) etc.

Types of Stem:

- Depending upon the size and woodiness, stems can be classified as: herbs, shrubs and trees.

1. Herbacious:

- These are plants with small and soft stems. They are either unbranched or have a few branches. These include *Brassica, Triticum, Raphanus sativus* (raddish) etc.

2. Shrubs:

- These are medium sized perennial plants with profusely branched woody stems. The branches arise from the base of the stem and the plants attain a bushy appearance. E.g., *Hibiscus rosa-sinensis, Camellia sinensis* (Tea plant).

3. Trees:

- These are Perennial plants with hard woody stems. They have a long trunk and branches arise from the upper part of the stem. E.g., *Magnifera indica*.

Branching in Stem:

- A branch may be defined as a lateral appendage arising from the axil of the leaf, differentiated into nodes and internodes. There are two main types of branching.
- **Lateral.**
- **Dichotomous.**

Lateral Branching:

- The branches are produced laterally from lateral buds present on the main axis. It is of following two types.
- **Cymose Branching:** The main axis terminates into a flower or a tendril and before its termination it gives off one or more lateral branches. Cymose branching is of three types.

- **Scorpoid Cyme:** If successive branches develop on alternate side to form a zig – zag structure e.g. *Vitis vinifera*.
- **Helicoid Cyme:** When the successive branches develop on one side only e.g., *Saraca indica*.
- **Biparous Cyme:** This is a cymose branching in which at each point two lateral branches develop at a time e.g., *Plumeria*.

- **Racemose or Indefinite Branching:** In this branching the main axis grows for indefinite period and during the course of its development regularly produces lateral branches in an acropetal order. Since there is single axis supporting lateral branches, this type of branching is also called monopodial branching e.g. *Polyalthia*.

Dichotomous Branching:
- The terminal bud divides into two each forming a branch likewise the tip of daughter branches also divide. Thus in dichotomous branching each branch bears two daughter branches. It is of following types.
- **Normal Dichotomy:** In this type both the daughter branches are of equal dimension e.g., *Psilotum, Lycopodium*.

- **Sympodial Dichotomy:** In this type two branches of dichotomy show unequal growth. Here one of the branches grows more vigorously while the other is suppressed. It is of two types.
- **Scorpioid Dichotomy:** The suppression takes place on alternate sides of successive branching.
- **Helecoid Dichotomy:** In this type branch of the same side is suppressed each time.

Modifications of Stem:
- In some plants, stems get modified to carry out some specific functions like storage of food Perennation, vegetative propagation etc. The various modifications of stem are:
- **Underground modification of stem.**
- **Sub – aerial modification of stem.**
- **Aerial modification of stem**

Rhizome:

- It is a thick, Prostrate and branched stem, growing horizontally beneath the soil surface. It has distinct nodes and internodes. The nodes bear small scale leaves with buds in their axil. These buds remain dormant and develop normal shoots during favourable conditions. The lower surface of node gives out adventitious roots e.g. *Zingiber officinale* (ginger), *Curcuma domestica* (turmeric).

Tuber:

- It is the swollen tip of underground branch. This branch arises from the axil of the leaf on the main stem. The tip of these branches becomes swollen due to accumulation of food material. The tubes are round or oval in shape. Each tuber has many notches on the surface called **eyes.** Tubers do not give off adventitious roots e.g. *Solanum.*

Corm:

- Corm is condensed form of rhizome growing vertically down into soil. It is spherical to oval in shape and branched. Internodes are usually reduced and one or more axillary buds are present in the axil of the scale leaves. Some of these buds grow into daughter corms. Corms bear adventitious roots either at the base or throughout the surface e.g. *Crocus sativus* (saffron), *Gladiolus,* etc.

Bulb:

- It is highly condensed stem, represented by a short convex or highly conical disc. On its upper surface are present large numbers of flashy scale leaves surround at terminal bud at the centre of the disc. The fleshy leaves of the bulb store food in the form of carbohydrates. A few outer leaves which become dry and scaly are protective in function. Large number of adventitious roots arise from lower surface e.g. *Allium cepa, A. sativum.*

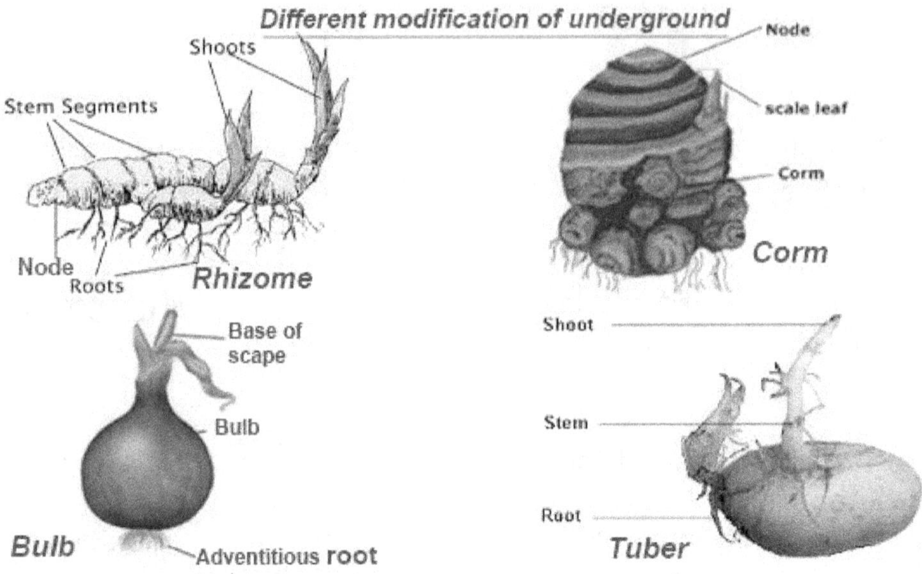

Runner or Sobole:

- It is a prostrate aerial stem creeping horizontally on the surface of the soil. It has long internodes. At each node axillary bud form aerial shoot and roots are given out at lower surface. E.g., *Cynodon*, *Oxalis*, etc.

Sucker:

- This is a sub – aerial branch arising from the basal underground portion of the main stem. Initially, it grows horizontally below the surface of the earth but soon grows obliquely upward forming a leafy shoot. Suckers are much shorter and stouter than runners. E.g., *Metha arvensis* (Podina).

Stolon:

- It is similar to runner but is sub–terranean. Stolon is produced at the base of the stem under the soil. It gives out branches in different directions which bear a bud at their tips. Each of these bud develop into a new plant e.g. *Dracaena* (dragon plant).

Offset:

- It is also similar to runner and originate from the axil of a leaf but has shorter and thicker internodes. It runs almost parallel to the surface, producing at its apex a tuft of leaves above and a cluster of small adventitious roots below e.g. *Pistia, Eichhorina* (water hyacinth).

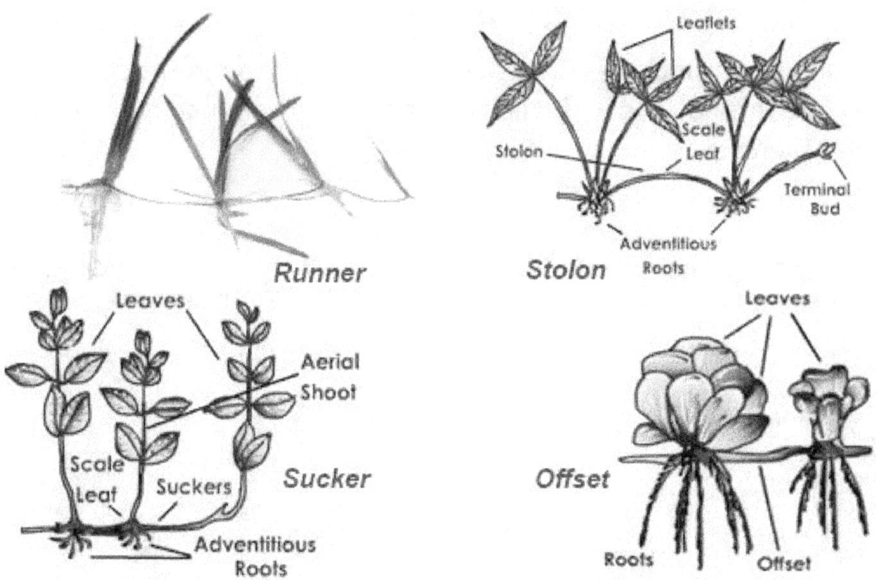

Aerial Modification of Stem:

Stem Tendril:

- In plants with weak aerial stem, some axillary buds, instead of developing into branches, from tendrils. These are thin, wiry, leafless spirally coiled structures which help the plant in climbing. *Vitis* (vine) – terminal bud terminates into tendril.

Thorne:

- It represents a auxiliary branch of limited growth. It is hard, often straight, pointed and may be branched. Thorns serve to be a defensive organ e.g. *Citrus* (lemon).

Phylloclade:

- Plants of dry arid habitats shed their leaves to reduce water loss. In such plants, stem or its branch become modified into flat, fleshy and green leaf – like structure with distinct nodes and internodes. These are known as phylloclades or cladophylls. Some bear modified leaves into the form of scales or spines. Phylloclades serve as organs of photosynthesis and storage.

Cladode:

- These are phylloclades made of only one or two internodes of a branch. Cladode are flat and leaf – like and perform the function of folage leaves e.g. *Asparagus*.

Bulbils:

- These are modified vegetative or floral buds arising in the axil of scale or foliage leaves. They grow into a new plant while still attached to the parent plant or after their separation e.g. *Dioscorea* (wild yam), *oxalis* etc.

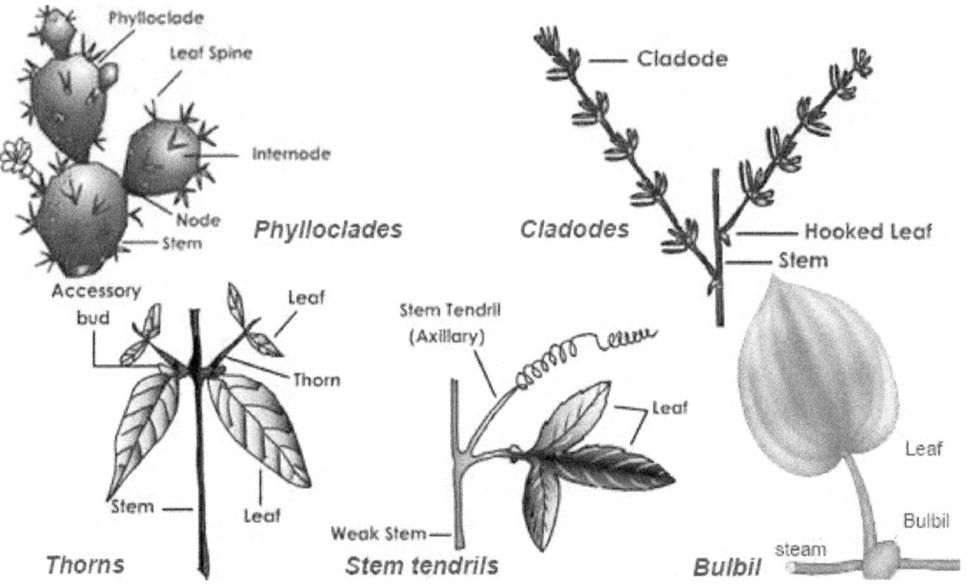

- **Primary Functions:**
- It bears leaves and holds them in such a position so as to provide maximum sunlight.
- The stem conducts water and mineral nutrients from the roots to the leaves, flowers and fruits.
- The stem conducts organic food from the leaves to the roots and storage organs.
- It holds flowers in such a position so as to facilitate pollination and fertilization.
- The stem also bears fruits and seeds.

- **Secondary or Accessory Functions:**
- **Storage:** In many species, the stem acts as an organ of storage of food material (e.g. rhizome of Ginger, tuber of Potato, water – phylloclade).
- **Synthesis of Food:** Some modified stems of xerophytic plants are green, flat and leaf – like. They perform photosynthesis e.g. *Opuntia, Asparagus*.
- **Perennation:** Underground modified stems of many plants (e.g. Ginger) tide over the unfavourable conditions and help in perennation.
- **Vegetative Propagation:** In many plants, stems serve as means of vegetative propagation e.g. tuber of Potato, corns etc.

Morphology of Leaf:

- Leaf may be defined as a flattened lateral outgrowth developing at the nodes of the stem and or branches in acropetal succession. A typical angiospermic leaf consists of three parts viz. leaf base, petiole and lamina.

- The basal part of leaf by which it is attached to the stem is called leaf base. Usually, it protects a small bud at its axil. In many legumes and some other plants, leaf base is swollen to form **pulvinus**. The sheathing leaf base of grass possesses a small leaf-like outgrowth called **ligule**, just below the lamina. The leaf with legule is termed as **ligulate**. In many species leaf base consists small out growths called **stipules** which protect the young leaves and the axillary bud. **Stipules** are usually found in dicotyledons. A leaf with stipules is called **stipulate** and a leaf without stipules is called **exstipulate**.

Petiole (Mesopodium):

- A petiole is a cylindrical or sub-cylindrical structure of a leaf which joins the lamina to the base. It raises the lamina above the level of stem so as to provide it with sufficient light exposure. A leaf with a petiole is **called petiolate** and the one without it is called **sessile**. When the petiole is short, the leaf is called **subsessile**.

Lamina (Epipodium) or Leaf Blade:

- The leaf lamina is normally a flat, thin, expanded and green structure where all the functions of leaf are carried on. It is a seat of photosynthesis, gaseous exchange, transpiration and most of the metabolic reactions of the plant. The shape, margin, apex, surface and extent of incision of lamina vary in different leaves.

- A lamina has two surfaces, **adaxial** or upper and **abaxial** or lower. Veins are **prominent over the abaxial surface** which is, therefore, also called **dorsal** or outer surface. Correspondingly adaxial surface is referred to as **ventral** or inner surface.

- A leaf where the two surfaces are distinct and the lamina lies horizontally is termed as **dorsiventral leaf.** When the distinction between the two surfaces is absent, the leaf is called **isobilateral.** A leaf is called **centric** if the blade is cylindrical or needle like, e.g., onion.

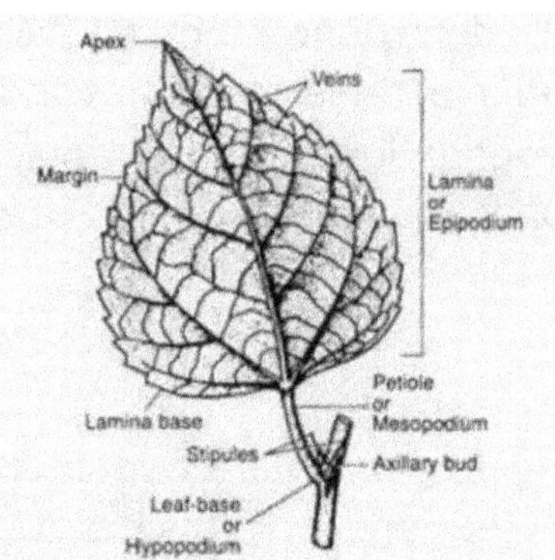

Phyllotaxy:

- The arrangement of leaves on the stem and its branches is called Phyllotaxy. It is of following three types.
- **Alternate or Spiral:** When single leaf is born at each node and the leaves are arranged in such a way that a line drawn on a stem through the leaf bases takes a spiral course, the arrangement is called alternate or spiral or acyclic. E.g., Mango. A Phyllotaxy is written by taking the number of spirals

(circles) as numerator and the number of leaves denominator. Thus spiral Phyllotaxy belong to following sub-types:

- **Distichous:** Two ranked (2) or in two vertical rows e.g. Graminae (Poaceal)
- **Tristichous:** Three ranked (3) or in two vertical rows e.g.Cyperaceae.
- **Pentastichous:** Five ranked (5) or in five vertical rows. *Hibiscus rosa-sinensis.*
- **Octostichous:** Eight ranked (8) or in eight vertical rows e.g. Papaya.

- **Opposite:** When pair of leaves arise at each node on opposite sides it is called opposite phyllotaxy. It is of two types.
- **Opposite Superposed:** All the pairs of leaves of a branch arise in the same plane so that only two vertical rows of leaves are formed. E.g., Guava.
- **Opposite decussate:** A pair of leaves at one node stands at right angles to the next upper or lower pair so that four vertical rows are formed on the stem. E.g. *Zinnia,* Tulsi, etc.

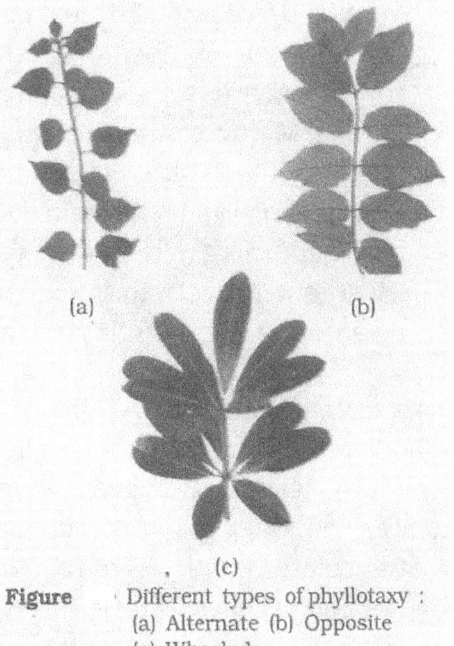

Figure Different types of phyllotaxy : (a) Alternate (b) Opposite (c) Whorled

- **Whorled or Verticillate:** In this case more than two leaves arise at each node forming a circle or whorl. E.g., *Alistonia scholaris.*

Venation

- The arrangement of principal Vein and veinlets in the lamina is termed as venation. The veins are chiefly made of vascular tissue, xylem and phloem. They have two important functions.
- Mechanical support to lamina and
- Supply of water and minerals (absorbed by roots) to all cells of the leaf and transport of organic food synthesized by green cells of the leaf to all non-green cells of the plant.

Types of Venation:
- There are following two types of venation.
- Parallel Venation.
- Reticulate Venation.

Parallel Venation: In this type veins run parallel to each other from base to the tip of lamina. It is characteristic of monocotyledons leaves. Parallel venation is of two types.
- **Parallel Unicostate:** The leaf lamina possesses single main vein which gives rise to large number of lateral veins. All the lateral veins run parallel towards margins. E.g. Banana.
- **Parallel Multicostate:** The leaf lamina possess several main veins which run parallel to each other. It is of two types.
- **Convergent Type:** The main vein runs parallel to each other and converges at the apex. E.g., grasses, wheat, bamboo.
- **Divergent Type:** In this type, principal vein arising from the tip of petiole, diverge towards margins of leaf blade in a more or less parallel manner.

Reticulate Venation: The pattern of venation in which veinlets are repeatedly branched and form a network is called reticulate venation. It is characteristic of dicotyledons leaves. However, some monocotyledonous leaves also show reticulate venation. E.g. *Dioscorea*.
- Reticulate venation is of following types.
- **Reticulate Unicostate:** In this type there is only one principal vein that gives off many lateral veins which run towards margins or apex of the leaf. E.g., mango.
- **Reticulate Multicostate:** In this type, there are two or more principal veins arising from the tip of petiole which run upward. It may be of two types.
- **Convergent type:** The main veins converge towards the apex of the lamina. E.g. smilax.
- **Divergent type:** The main veins diverge towards the margins e.g. *Cucurbita*

Furcate venation: The veins neither run parallel nor form reticulations. They are dichotomously branched. e.g., *Circeaster*. It is characteristic of ferns

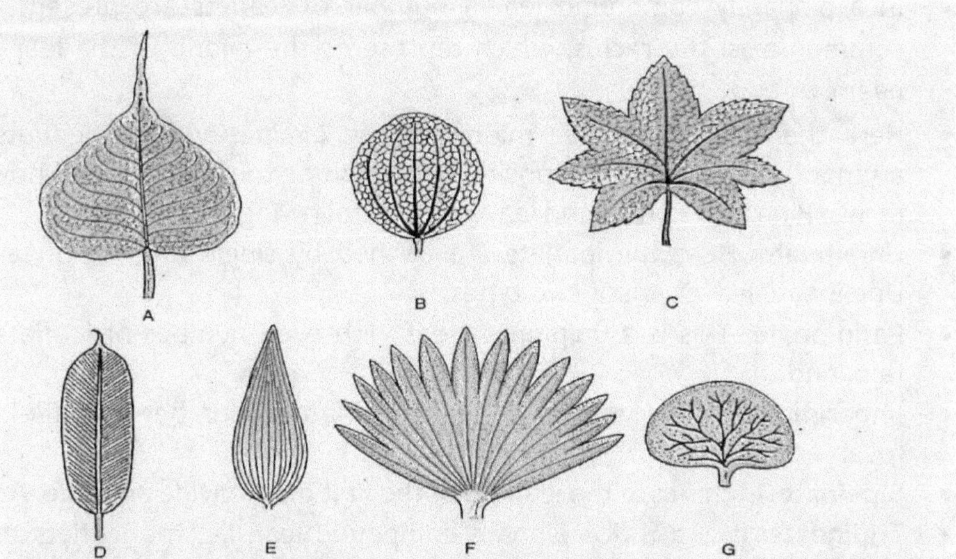

Types of Venation. A, reticulate unicostate venation of Peepal (*Ficus religiosa*). B, reticulate multicostate convergent of *Zizyphus*. C, reticulate multicostate divergent of *Cuurbita*. D, parallel unicostate in *Musa* (Banana). E, parallel multicostate convergent of Bamboo. F, parallel multicostate of Fan Palm. G, furcate venation.

Types of Leaves:

- On the basis of incision (cutting) of lamina, leaves are grouped into two categories:

1. Simple Leaf

2. Compound Leaf

- **Simple Leaf:** A leaf is said to be simple, when its lamina is entire or when incised, the incisions do not touch the midrib or petiole e.g. mango, banyan, etc.
- **Compound Leaf:** When the incisions of lamina reach upto the midrib breaking it into a number of leaflets, the leaf is called compound. A bud is present in the axil of petiole in both simple and compound leaves, but not in the axil of leaflets of the compound leaf.

Depending upon the position of leaflets, the compound leaves are divided into following two types.

- **Pinnately compound leaves.**
- **Palmately compound leaves.**

Pinnately Compound Leaves:

- In a pinnately compound leaf a number of leaflets are present on a common axis, the **rachis,** which represents the midrib of the leaf as in neem.
- Here the incision reaches midrib of the lamina, and the leaflets are arranged in alternate or opposite manner along the midrib, now known as rachis. Pinnately compound leaves are of following types.
- **Unipinnate:** Here the leaflets are formed by single division of lamina. Unipinnate leaves are of two types:
- **Paripinnate:** This is a unipinnate leaf with even number of leaflets e.g. tamarind.
- **Imparipinnate:** This unipinnate leaf bearing odd number of leaflets e.g. rose.
- **Bipinnate:** In this case the leaflets of the first order divide again i.e. Acacia.
- **Tripinnate:** It is a thrice pinnate compound leaf, i.e. the leaflets of the second order divide once more e.g., *Moringa*.
- **Decompound:** This is a pinnately compound leaf were incision of lamina occurs more than three times e.g. carrot.

Palmately Compound Leaf:

- In palmately compound leaves, the leaflets are attached to a common point, i,e. at the tip of petiole, as in silk, cotton

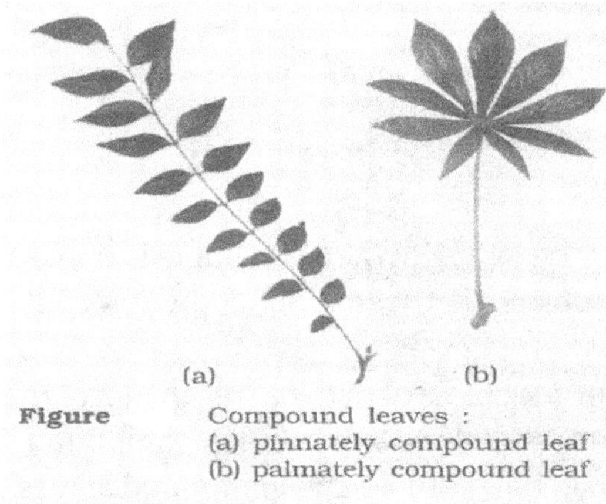

Figure Compound leaves :
(a) pinnately compound leaf
(b) palmately compound leaf

- In this type the incision of lamina is directed towards its base. The leaflets are attached to the tip of the petiole. Palmately Compound leaves are of following types:
- **Unifoliate:** This palmalety compound leaf has a single leaflet articulated to the apex of a winged Petiole e.g. *Citrus*.

- **Bifoliate:** In this type two leaflets are articulated to the petiole e.g., *Bignonia grandiflora*.
- **Trifoliate:** Three leaflets are articulated to the tip of Petiole e.g., *oxalis*.

- **Quadrifoliate:** In this type, four leaflets are articulated to the tip of Petiole e.g., *Marsilea*.
- **Multifoliate (Digitate):** Four or more leaflets are articulated to the tip of the petiole, spreading like fingers from the palm e.g. *Bombax*.

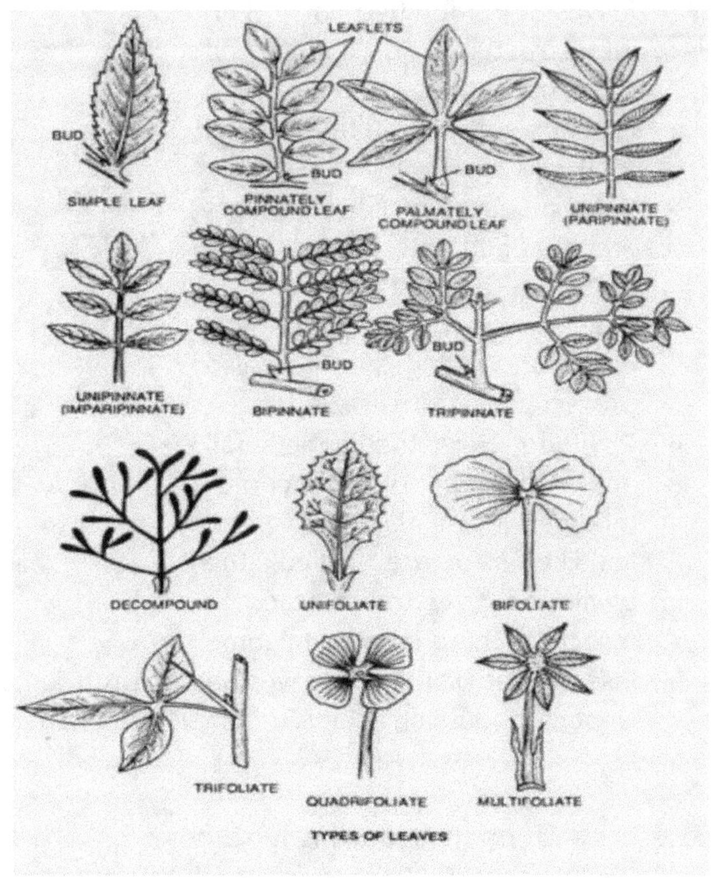

Difference between Pinnately Compound leaf and a Palmately Compound leaf:

Pinnately compound leaf	Palmately compound leaf
Many numbers of leaflets are present on a common axis	Several leaflets are attached to a common point.
Leaflets are attached to common axis called rachis	Leaflets are attached to a common point on the leaf stalk.
Leaflet bearing axis is the continuation of the petiole	Leaflet bearing axis is very short.
Ex: Neem leaves	Ex: Cotton leaves

Modification of Leaves:

- **Storage Leaves:** Some plants of dry habitats commonly have strongly thickened succulent leaves with water storage regions e.g., members of Crassulaceae.

- **Leaf Tendril:** In some plants leaves are modified into then wiry structures. The coil around the support and help the plant in climbing e.g. entire life modified as in wild pea.
- **Spines:** Leaves of certain plants are modified into spines as in cacti (e.g. opuntia), which is an adaptation to xerophytic conditions. Besides spines also protect plant from grazing.
- **Phyllode:** Here the leaflets fall and the petiole becomes modified into a flattened green leaf-like structure called the phyllode e.g. Australian acacia.
- **Insect Catching Leaves:** In some insectivores plants the leaves are adapted to catch and digest insects. In Nepenthes, lamina itself is modified into pitcher.

Leaf tendril

Leaves modified into spines

Fleshy leaves

(a) (b) (c)

Figure Modifications of leaf for : (a) support: tendril (b) protection: spines (c) storage: fleshy leaves

Functions of leaves:

The leaves perform the following functions:

- **Photosynthesis:** Photosynthesis is the primary function of leaves. They convert carbon dioxide, water, and UV light into glucose through the process of photosynthesis.
- **Transpiration:** Transpiration is the removal of excess water from the plants into the atmosphere. This occurs by the opening of stomata present in the leaves.
- **Guttation:** Removal of excess water from the xylem at the edges of the leaves when the stomata are closed is known as guttation.
- **Storage:** Leaves are a site of photosynthesis. Therefore, they store water and nutrients. The succulent and thick leaves particularly adapt to water storage.
- **Defence:** Some leaves are modified into spines to protect them from being damaged or eaten by animals. For eg., *Opuntia*.
- **Reproduction:** Leaves of some plants like *Bryophyllum* sprout new plants. The leaves of this plant begin the process of mitosis and asexually reproduce in the form of plantlets that cover the edges of the leaf.

Inflorescence:

- The arrangement of flowers on the floral axis is termed as **inflorescence.** A flower is a modified shoot wherein the shoot apical meristem changes to floral meristem. Internodes do not elongate and the axis gets condensed. The apex produces different kinds of floral appendages laterally at successive nodes instead of leaves. When a shoot tip transforms into a flower. It is solitary. Depending on whether the apex gets converted into a flower or continues to grow, two major types of inflorescences are defined – raecmose and cymose.

Racemose inflorescence:_ In raecmose type of inflorescences the main axis continues to grow, the flowers are borne laterally in an **acropetal succession** as shown in figure below. Racemose inflorescence is of following types:

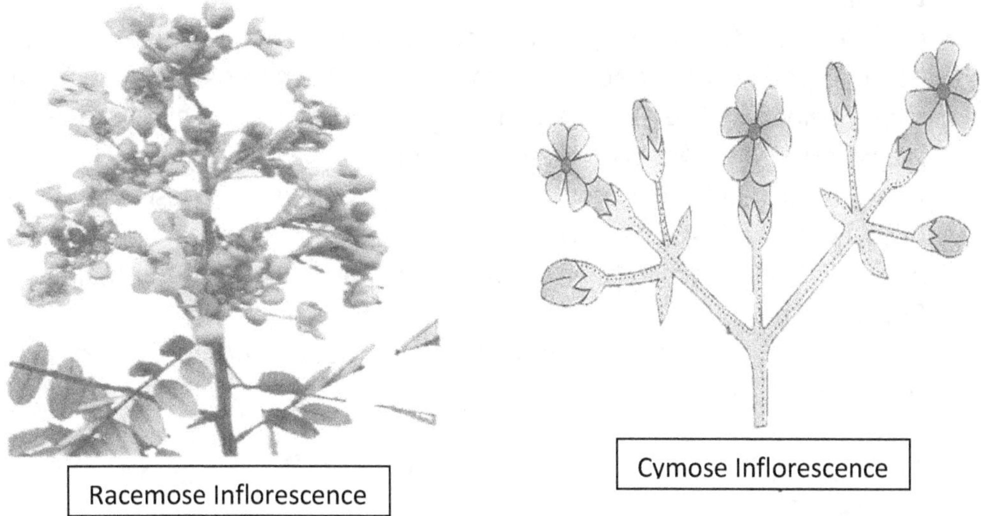

Racemose Inflorescence

Cymose Inflorescence

- **Raceme:** The inflorescence axis is simple, elongated bears stalked flowers e.g. *Brassica.*
- **Panicle:** It is modified raceme. Here main inflorescence axis is branched and flowers are born acropetally on lateral branches, also called compound raceme e.g. *Yucca* (Gold mohur).
- **Spike:** It is similar to raceme but the flowers are sessile e.g. *Piper longum* etc.
- **Compound Spike (Spikelet or Locusta):** The inflorescence axis is branched and the flowers are arranged in a spike like manner e.g., *Amaranthus.* In grasses the unit of compound inflorescence is spikelet. Each spikelet is

composed of a cluster of one or more flowers and their associated brackets.

- **Strobile:** It is a spike in which each flower is borne in the axil of a persistant membranous bracket e.g. *Humulus lupulus.*
- **Catkin (Amentum):** It is a spike consisting of unisexual flowers. The inflorescence is long and pendulous e.g. *Morus, Salix* etc.
- **Spadix:** It is a spike with thick and fleshy inflorescence axis surrounding by one or several brightly coloured brackets, called spathe e.g. banana, maize.
- **Corymb:** It is a racemose inflorescence with shortened main axis. The flowers have unequal stalks. The lower flower have much longer pedicel than the upper ones, bringing all the flowers to more or less same line e.g. *Prunus cerasus* (cherry).
- **Compound Corymb:** In this case the central axis is branched and the flowers are born on these branches in Corymb like manner e.g. *Pyrus torminalis.*
- **Umbel:** The inflorescence axis is shortened but the individual flowers are born on pedicels of about the same length. All the flowers arise from the single point, like the ribs of an umbrella. At the base of flower stalks, there is a whorl of brackets forming the involucres, e.g., Allium *Cepa.*
- **Compound Umbel:** Compound umbel where inflorescence axis is branched, the branches arise from a single point in exactly umbel like manner. The branches bear umbels which are known as Umbellules, e.g. *Daucos carota.*
- **Capitate:** In this case large number of sessile flowers arise from a suppressed axis forming a globose structure, e.g., *Mimosa.*

- **Capitulum or Head (Anthodium):** The inflorescence axis is flattened forming a convex disc, called receptacle. A large number of sessile flower called florets are born on the receptacle e.g. sunflower.

Cymose inflorescence: In cymose type of inflorescence the main axis terminates in a flower, hence is limited in growth. The flowers are borne in a **basipetal order**. This is of following three types.

- **Uniparous or Monochasal Cyme:** This is an inflorescence where the main axis terminates into flower, and produces only one lateral branch which also terminates into flower. It can be:
- **Scorpoid Cyme (cincinnus):** When successive lateral branches develop on alternate sides in a zig-zag manner, e.g., *Ranunculus bulbosus*.

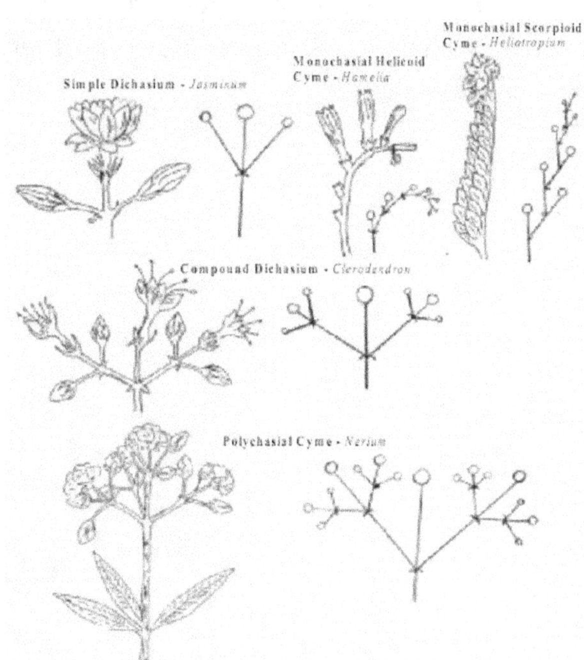

- **Helicoid Cyme (Drepmium or Bostryx):** When lateral branches develop on the same side forming a sort of helix, e.g. *Juncus*.
- **Biparous or Dichasial Cyme:** In this type, the main axis terminates into flower and produces two lateral branches, e.g., *Ixora*.
- **Multiporous or Polychasial Cyme:** This is a Cymose inflorescence in which main axis is terminated by a flower and produces many lateral branches, each terminating into flower, e.g., *Calotropis*.

Difference between Racemose and Cymose inflorescence:

Racemose inflorescence	Cymose inflorescence
Inflorescence in which young flowers are present at the tip and older flowers are arranged at the base	Inflorescence in which old flowers are present at the tip and young flowers are arranged at the base
Main axis continues to grow and produce flowers laterally.	The main axis has limited growth which terminates into flower.

Flower:

- Flower may be defined as modified shoot meant essentially meant for the reproduction of plant. The flower usually develops from a bud, growing axil of a small leaf like structure known as bract. The flower is the reproductive unit in the angiosperms.
- A typical flower has four different kinds of whorls arranged successively on the swollen end of the stalk or pedicel, called thalamus or receptacle. These are **calyx, corolla, androecium** and **gynoecium.** Calyx and corolla are **accessory organs**, while androecium and gynoecium are **reproductive organs.**
- In some flowers like lily, the calyx and corolla are not distinct and are termed as **perianth.** When a flower has both androecium and gynoecium, it is **bisexual.** A flower having either only stamens or only carpels is **unisexual.**

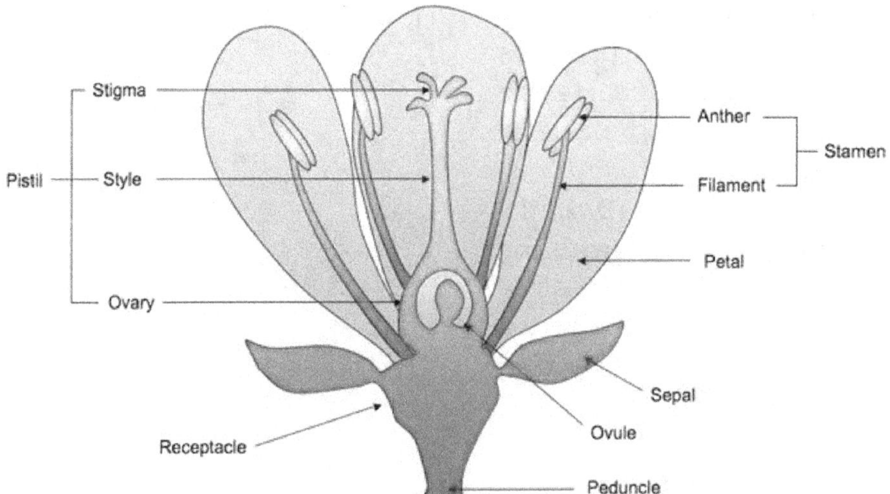

- **Symmetry:** In symmetry, the flower may be **actinomorphic** (radial symmetry) or **zygomorphic** (bilateral symmetry).
- **Actinomorphic:** When a flower can be divided into two equal radial halves in any radial plane passing through the centre, it is said to be actinomorphic, e.g., mustard, datura, chilli.
- **Zygomorphic:** When a flower can be divided into two similar halves only in one particular vertical plane, it is zygomorphic, e.g., pea, gulmohur, bean, cassia.

- **Asymmetric:** A flower is asymmetric (irregular) if it cannot be divided into two similar halves by any vertical plane passing through the centre, as in **canna.**
- **Number of Floral appendages:** A flower may be **trimerous, tetramerous** or **pentamerous** when the floral appendages are in multiple of 3, 4 and 5, respectively. **Bracts:** Flowers with bracts (reduced leaf found at the base of the pedicel) are called **bracteate** and those without bracts, **ebracteate.**
- **Position of floral whorls:** Based on the position of calyx, corolla and androecium in respect of the ovary on thalamus, the flowers are described as **hypogynous, perigynous** and **epigynous** (as shown in figure below).
- **Hypogynous:** In the hypogynous flower the gynoecium occupies the highest position while the other parts are situated below it. The ovary in such flowers is said to be **superior.** E.g., mustard, China rose and brinjal.
- **Perigynous:** If gynoecium is situated in the centre and other parts of the flower are located on the rim of the thalamus almost at the same level, it is called perigynous. The ovary here is said to be **half inferior.** E.g., plum, rose, peach.
- **Epigynous:** In epigynous flowers, the margin of thalamus grows upward enclosing the ovary completely and getting fused with it, the other parts of flower arise above the ovary. Hence, the ovary is said to be **inferior** as in flowers of guava and cucumber, and the ray florets of sunflower.

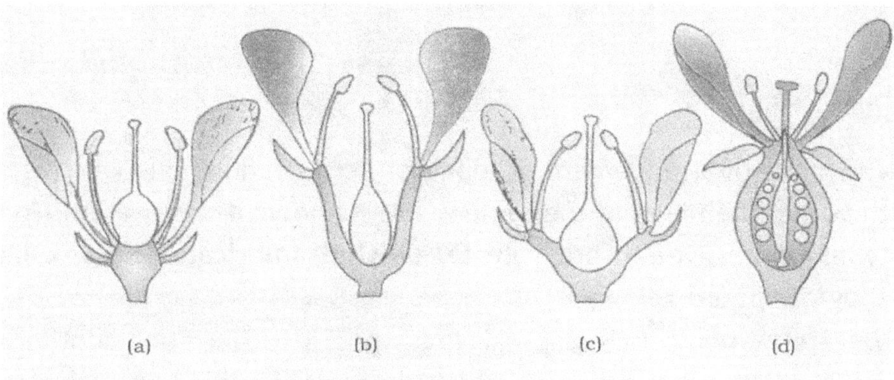

(a)   (b)   (c)   (d)

Figure . Position of floral parts on thalamus : (a) Hypogynous (b) and (c) Perigynous (d) Epigynous

Structure of a flower:

Each flower normally has four floral whorls, viz., calyx, corolla, androecium and gynoecium (as shown in figure below).

Calyx:

- It is the outer most floral whorl consisting of **Sepals**. Sepals are green and protective in function. If sepals are free, the condition is called **Polysepalous**, and if fused the condition is called **gamosepalous**, e.g, *Hibiscus*.

Corolla:

- It is the second floral whorl consisting of Petals. Like Sepals, Petals may be free (**Polypetalous**) or fused (**gamopetalous**). They are brightly coloured due to the presence of **anthocyanin** and **anthoxanthin** pigments. Petals are usually differentiated into a lower narrow stalk-like portion, the claw and the upper expanded portion the limb. The primary function of a corolla is to attract insects for Pollination. The shape and color of corolla vary greatly in plants. Corolla may be tubular, bell – shaped, funnel – shaped or wheel – shaped

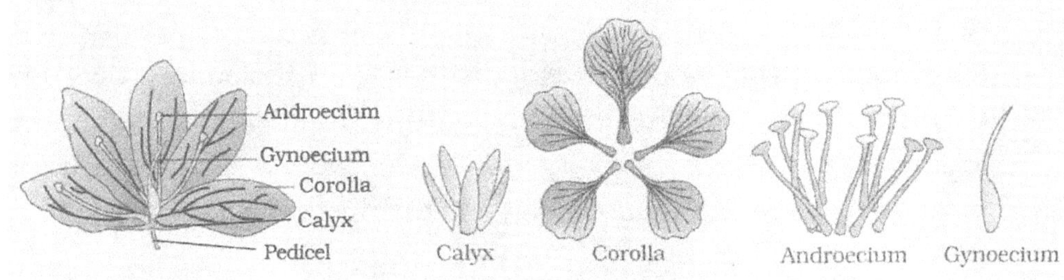

Aestivation:

- The mode of arrangement of sepals or petals in floral bud with respect to the other members of the same whorl is known as aestivation. The main types of aestivation are **valvate, twisted, imbricate** and **vexillary** (as shown in figure below).
- <u>Valvate:</u> When sepals or petals in a whorl just touch one another at the margin, without overlapping, as in *Calotropis*, it is said to be valvate.
- <u>Twisted:</u> If one margin of the appendage overlaps that of the next one and so on as in chine rose, lady's finger and cotton, it is called twisted.
- <u>Imbricate:</u> If the margins of sepals or petals overlap one another but not in any particular direction as in cassia and gulmohur, aestivation is called imbricate.

- **<u>Vexillary:</u>** In pea and bean flowers, there are five petals, the largest (standard) overlaps the two lateral petals (wings) which in turn overlap the two smallest anterior petals (keel) this type of aestivation is known as **vexillary or papilionaceous.**

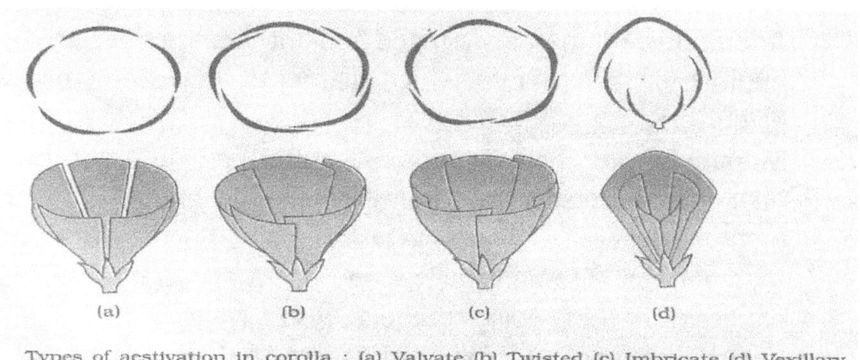

Figure   Types of aestivation in corolla : (a) Valvate (b) Twisted (c) Imbricate (d) Vexillary

Androecium:

- Androecium is composed of stamens. Each stamen which represents the male reproductive organ. Each stamen, also called microsporophyll is made of three parts:
- **Filament:** Filament is a slender stalk, bearing at its tip sac like anther.
- **Anther:** A typical anther is dithecous, because it has two elongate lobes which are united throughout their length by connective. Each lobe has two chambers, the **pollen-sacs.** The pollen grains are produced in pollen sacs. A sterile stamen is called **staminode.**

- **Connective:** The connection between two anther lobes is the connective

- Stamens of flower may be united with other members such as petals or among themselves. When stamens are attached to the petals, they are **epipetalous** as in brinjal, or **epiphyllous** when attached to the perianth as in the flowers of lily.

- The stamens in a flower may either remain free (**polyandrous**) or may be united in varying degrees. The stamens may be united into one bunch or one bundle (**monoadelphous**) as in China rose, or two bundles (**diadelphous**) as in pea, or into more than two bundles (**polyadelphous**) as in *citrus*. There may be a variation in the length of filaments within a flower, as in salvia

Cohesion of Stamens:

- Fusion amongst the members of same whorl is called cohesion. Following types of cohesions takes place in stamens.
- **Polyandrous:** The stamens are free from one another, e.g., *Ranunculus, Papaver* etc.
- **Adelphous:** Filaments are fused and anthers are free. Depending upon the number of groups into which filaments are fused, following types are given:
- **Monadelphous:** The stamens are united at one group by fusion of their filaments anthers, anthers being free, e.g., *Hibiscus*. This is characteristic of family Malvaceae.
- **Diadelphous:** Stamens are fused in two bundles by fusion of their filaments, anthers being free, e.g., *Pisum* (Pea).
- **Polyadelphous:** Condition in which stamens form more than ten bundles.
- **Syngenesious:** This is a condition in which statements are united by their anthers only; filaments remain free, as in family compositae (e.g. sunflower).
- **Synandrous:** Stamens are united throughout their length, e.g., *Curcurbita*.

Adhesion of Stamens:

Fusion of the members of two different whorls (e.g. Petals and Stamens etc) is known as adhesion. Following are some of the conditions.

- **Epipetalous:** Stamen adhere to the Petals wholly or partially by their filaments (anthers remaining free), e.g., *Ocimum, Solanum*, etc.
- **Epitepalous:** The stamens adhere to the tepals by their filaments only, e.g., *Asphodelus*.
- **Gynandrous:** The Stamens adhere to the carpels either throughout their length or by their anthers only, e.g., *Calotropis* (madar).

Gynoecium or pistil:

Gynoecium is the female reproductive part of the flower and is made up of one or more carpels. A carpel consists of three parts namely stigma, style and ovary. Ovary is the enlarged basal part, on which lies the elongated tube, the style. The style connects the ovary to the stigma. The stigma is usually at the tip of the style and is the receptive surface for pollen grains. Gynoecia could be broadly classified into two types.

- **Simple or Monocarpellary:** This condition is found in pea and other legumes where gynoecium is made up of only one carpel.
- **Compound or Multicarpellary:** It is made up of more than one carpel. Such a gynoecium is found in large number of angiosperms. Multicarpellary gynoecium could be of following types.
- **Apocarpous:** Each carpel is free from the other forming a separate gynoecium, e.g., *Ranunculus* etc.
- **Syncarpous:** All the carpels are fused with one another forming a compound gynoecium e.g. *Solanum*.

Number of Carpels:

Depending upon the number of Carpels a syncarpous gynoecium may be of following types.

- **Bicarpellary** – with two carpel e.g. *Coriandrum* (Coriander).
- **Tricarpellary** – with three carpels, e.g., *Allium cepa*.
- **Tetracarpellary** – with four carpels, e.g. *Berberis*.
- **Pentacarpellary** – with five carpels e.g. *Hibiscus* (shoe flower).
- **Multicarpellary** – with many carpels e.g. *Papaver*.

Chambers in the Ovary:

In monocarpellary gynoecium the ovary has only one chamber or locule. In apocarpous gynoecium each carpel has one locule. In syncarpous gynoecium the ovary may either have one or many locules. Depending upon the number of locules, following types of ovaries can be recognised.

- **Unilocular** – Ovary with one chamber, e.g., Pea.
- **Bilocular** – Ovary with two chambers, e.g., *Solanum*.
- **Trilocular** – Ovary with three chambers, e.g., *Musa*.
- **Tetralocular** – Ovary with four chambers e.g., *Ocimum*.
- **Pentalocular** – Ovary with five chambers e.g., *Hibiscus*.
- **Multilocular**- Ovary with many chambers e.g., *Citrus*.

Difference between Apocarpous and Syncarpous ovary:

Apocarpous ovary	Syncarpous ovary
In apocarpous ovary, two or more carpels are free	In syncarpous ovary, two or more carpels are fused
Example: Lotus	Example : mustard

Placentation:

The arrangement of ovules within the ovary is known as placentation. The placentation are of different types namely, marginal, axile, parietal, basal, central and free central (as shown in figure below).

Marginal: In marginal placentation the placenta forms a ridge along the ventral suture of the ovary and the ovules are borne on this ridge forming two rows, as in pea.

Axile: The placenta is axial when the ovules are attached to it in a multilocular ovary, the placentation is said to be axile, as in chine rose, tomato and lemon.

Parietal: In parietal placentation, the ovules develop on the inner wall of the ovary or on peripheral part. Ovary is one – chambered but it becomes two – chambered due to the formation of the **false septum**, e.g., mustard and argemone.

Free central: When the ovules are borne on central axis and septa are absent, as in dianthus and primrose the placentation is called free central.

Basal: In basal placentation, the placenta develops at the base of ovary and a single ovule is attached to it, as in sunflower, marigold.

Superficial: It is similar to axile placentation but the ovule bearing Placenta are born on the inner surface of the partition walls of multilocular ovary, e.g., *Nymphea*

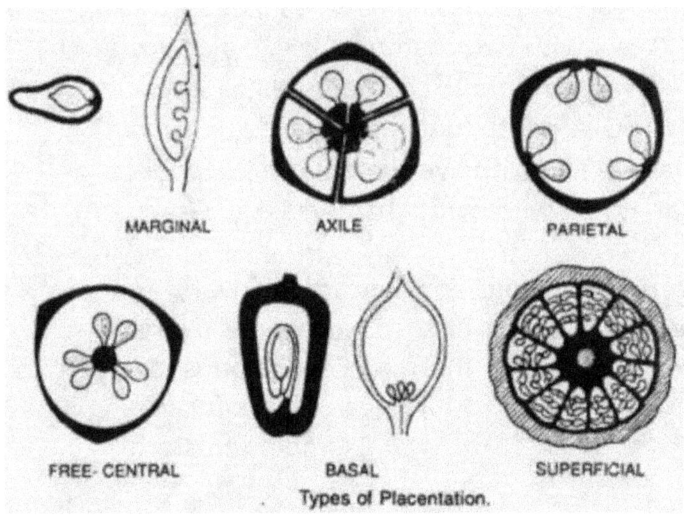

Types of Placentation.

Morphology of Fruit

- Fruit may be defined as a ripened ovary containing one or more seeds. Fruits are the main features of a flowering plant. It is a matured ovary that develops after fertilisation. Some fruits are developed without fertilization and are known as **parthenocarpic fruits**. In some fruits, the edible portion is not derived from the ovary, but rather from the aril, such as the mangosteen or pomegranate, and the pineapple from which tissues of the flower and stem provide food. Depending upon the part of the flower, fruits are of two types:

- **True Fruit**
- **False fruit**

True Fruit: The fruits that are formed from the ovary, such fruits are known as true fruits.

False Fruits: when other floral parts such as thalamus as in apple, pear, fig, calyx (as in pine apple), etc., form a major part of the fruit, such fruits are described as false fruits, accessory fruits or spurious fruits.

Structure of the Fruit:

Fruit consists of two main parts:

- **The Seeds:** developing from the ovules.
- **The Pericarp:** The pericarp (fruit wall) that develops from the wall of the ovary.

Structure of pericarp: It varies greatly in different kinds of fruits. In fruits such as Peaches, Plums and Cherries pericarp is clearly differentiated into three layers; the outer **epicarp**, the middle **mesocarp** and the inner **endocarp**. Of these, the epicarp and endocarp are usually one cell thick layers while the mesocarp may be very thin or may form a well-developed fleshy tissue, several centimetres thick.

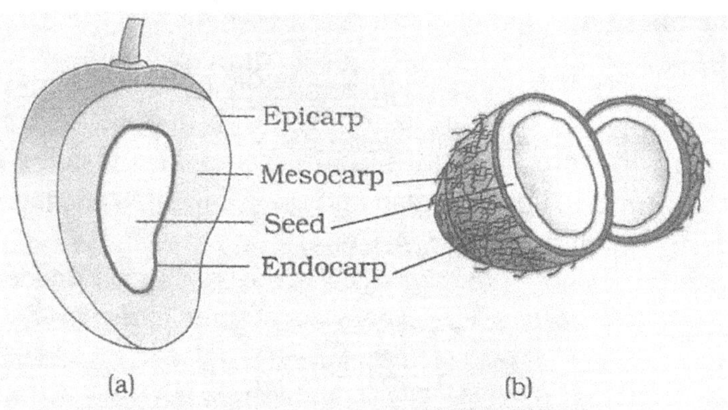

Types of Fruits:
- Simple fruits.
- Aggregate fruits.
- Composite fruits.

Simple Fruits:

A fruit that develops from a single ovary either monocarpellary or multicarpellary and syncarpous is said to be simple fruit. They may be sub -divided into dry fruits and fleshy fruits.

- **Dry Fruits:** In these fruits the pericarp becomes more or less dry when ripe. Dry fruits are of three types – dehiscent, indehiscent and schizocarpic fruits.
- **Dehiscent fruits:** burst automatically on ripening, liberating seeds. *Pisum* (Paplionaceae).
- **Indehiscent Fruits**: do not brust automatically on ripening. Their seeds are discharged after the decay of pericarp, e.g., *Zea mays*.
- **Schizocarpic Fruits**: splits into number of indehiscent units called mericarps. Each mericarp contains one or more seeds. However, the pericarp does not brust and seeds are liberated only after the decomposition of Pericarp e.g. *Arachis hypogaea* (ground nut).
- **Fleshy Fruits:** Fruits in which the entire pericarp or part of it and or accessory structures associated with it becomes fleshy and juicy at maturity, e.g., *Prunus amygdalis* (almond).

Aggregate Fruits:
- Fruits developed from a flower having a number of free carpels, all of which ripe together and are aggregated as a unit on a common receptacle are known as aggregate fruits. The fruitlets of a group are collectively termed as eterio, e.g., blackberry (*Rubus*).

Multiple or Composite Fruits:
- These fruits are the products of the whole inflorescence together with its component parts. They are composed of a number of closely associated fruits derived from the entire inflorescence and forming one composite fruit at maturity. These are also known as infrutescence, e.g., *Morus indica* (Mulbery), *Ananas comosus* (Ananas).

Functions of Fruit:

1. Edible part of the fruit is a source of food, energy for animals.
2. They are source of many chemicals like sugar, pectin, organic acids, vitamins and minerals.
3. The fruit protects the seeds from unfavourable climatic conditions and animals.
4. Both fleshy and dry fruits help in the dispersal of seeds to distant places.
5. In certain cases, fruit may provide nutrition to the developing seedling.
6. Fruits provide source of medicine to humans.

Morphology of Seed:

- Seed may be defined as a fertilized mature ovule with viable embryo. It usually stores food material and has a protective coat. After fertilization, changes occur in various parts of the ovule and transforms into a seed.

Structure of Seed:

A mature seed consists of two essential parts:

- **The seed coat**
- **The embryo.**

The Seed Coat:

- The outer covering of seed is called **seed coat**. In most of the seeds, the seed coat is made up of two layers. The outer layer is called testa and the inner layer is called tegmen. The testa is usually thick and leathery while tegmen is thin, papery and fused with the testa. The function of the seed coat is to protect the delicate embryo within.
- The seed remains attached to the ovary wall or fruit wall (pericarp) by a short stalk called seed stalk or **funiculus**. In mature seeds the position of seed stalk is represented by a small oval depression called **hilum**. Just below the hilum is a small pore, the **micropyle.** In some seeds, the stalk is continuous with the seed coat and this fused part appears as small **ridge** just above the hilum. This ridge is known as **raphe.**

Embryo:

- The embryo may be defined as the young or miniature plant, enclosed within the seed coat. It develops from a fertilized egg. The embryo of a mature seed consists of four distinct parts.
- **Cotyledons.**
- **Plumule.**
- **Hypocotyl**
- **Radicle.**

Cotyledon: The Cotyledons are also known as seed leaves are attached to embryonic axis. Dicotyledons have two cotyledons which are situated opposite to each other, while as monocotyledons have only one cotyledon.

Plumule: The part of the embryonal axis lying immediately above the point of attachment of the cotyledons is known as epicotyls and at the tip of epicotyl lies the plumule.

Hypocotyl: The part of the embryonic axis below the point of attachment of the cotyledon is known as hypocotyls. It represents the root stem transition region, i.e. the part where stem changes into root.

Radicle: The radicle is the basal tip of the hypocotyls. When seed germinates, the radical becomes the primary root of the seedling.
The radicle, plumule and hypocotyl together form the embryonic axis or **tigellum.**

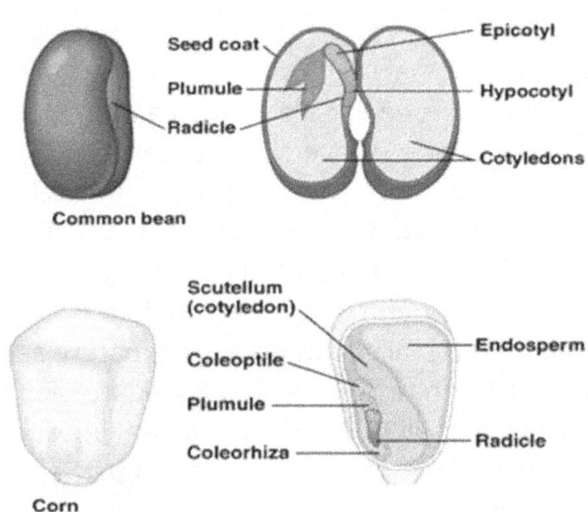

Classification of Seeds:
Based on the number of cotyledons present two types of seed are recognized.
- **Dicotyledonous seed:** Seeds with two cotyledons.
- **Monocotyledonous seed:** Seeds with one cotyledon

Based on the presence or absence of the endosperm the seed is of two types:
- **Albuminous or Endospermous Seeds.**
- **Ex-albuminous or non-endospermous seeds.**

Albuminous or Endospermous Seeds: The cotyledons are thin, membranous and mature seeds have endosperm persistent and nourishes the seedling during its early development.
Examples are; Castor, Sunflower, maize

Ex-albuminous or non-endospermous seeds: Food is utilised by the developing embryo and so the mature seeds are without endosperm. In such seeds, cotyledons store food and become thick and fleshy. Examples are; Pea. Groundnut

Functions of Seeds:
1. Seed encloses and protects the embryo for next generation.
2. It contains food for the development of embryo.
3. It is a means for the dispersal of new individuals of the species.
4. A seed is a means for the perpetuation of species. It may lie dormant during unfavourable conditions but germinates on getting suitable conditions.
5. Seeds of various plants are used as food, both for animals and men.
6. They are the basis of agriculture.
7. Seeds are the products of sexual reproduction, so they provide genetic variations and recombination in plants.

Structure of a dicotyledonous seed:

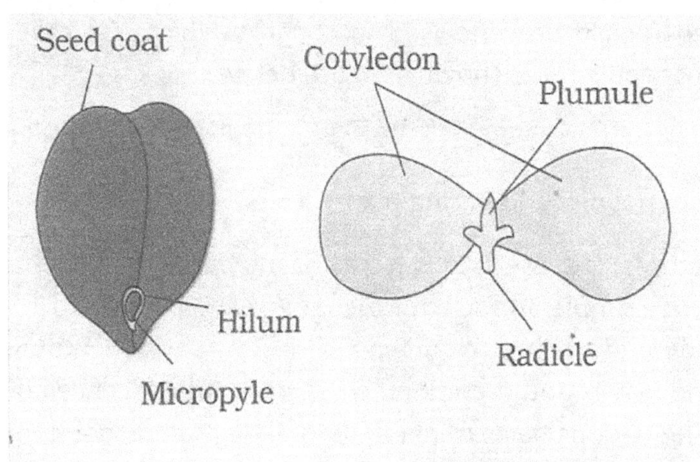

The outermost covering of a seed is the seed coat. The seed coat has two layers, the outer **testa** and the inner **tegmen**. The hilum is a scar on the seed coat through which the developing seeds were attached to the fruit. Above the hilum is a small pore called the **micropyle.** Within the seed coat is the embryo, consisting of an embryonal axis and two cotyledons. The cotyledons are often fleshy and full of reserve food materials. At the two ends of the embryonal axis are present the radicle and the plumule. In some seeds such as castor the endosperm formed as a result of double fertilisation, is a food storing tissue. In plants such as bean, gram and pea, the endosperm is not present in mature seeds and such seeds are called non – **endospermous**

Structure of monocotyledonous seed:

Generally, monocotyledonous seeds are **endospermic** but some as in orchids are non – endospermic. In the seeds of cereals such as maize the seed coat is membranous and generally fused with the fruit wall. The endosperm is bulky and stores food. The outer covering of endosperm separates the embryo by a **proteinous** layer called **aleurone** layer. The embryo is small and situated in a groove at one end of the endosperm. It consists of one large and shield shaped cotyledon known as **scutellum** and a short axis with a plumule and a radicle. The plumule and radicle are enclosed in sheaths which are called coleoptile and coleorhiza respectively (as shown in figure below).

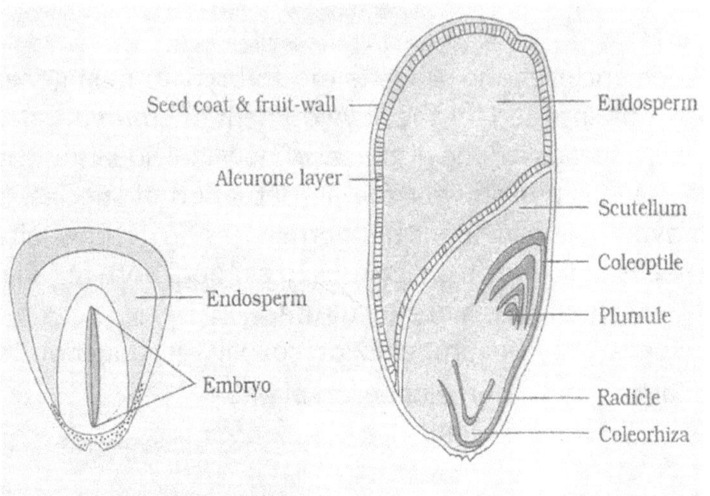

Semi-technical description of a typical flowering plant:-

Various morphological features are used to describe a flowering plant. The description has to be brief, in a simple and scientific language and presented in a proper sequence. The plant is described beginning with its habit, vegetative characters – roots, stem and leaves and then floral characters inflorescence and flower parts. After describing various parts of plant, a floral diagram and a floral formula are presented.

Floral formula:

- It is a symbolic representation of presence or absence of various floral organs, floral symmetry, sexuality, number, cohesion or adhesion as well as relationship of various floral organs and superior or inferior nature of ovary.
- The floral formula is represented by some symbols. In the floral formula,

(i)	Br : Bracteate		(ii)	Ebr : Ebracteate
(iii)	Brl : Bracteolate		(iv)	Ebrl : Ebracteolate
(v)	⊕ : Actinomorphic		(vi)	┼ : Zygomorphic
(vii)	☿ or ↥ : Staminate or Male		(viii)	♀ : Pistillate or Female
(ix)	☿ : Perfect, bisexual or hermaphrodite		(x)	N : Neuter.
(xi)	K : Calyx		(xii)	C : Corolla
(xiii)	P : Perianth		(xiv)	A : Androecium
(xv)	G : Gynoecium		(xvi)	Std : Staminode.

- Fusion is indicated by enclosing the figure within bracket and adhesion by a line drawn provides information about the number of parts of a flower, their arrangement and the relation they have with one another. The position of the mother axis with respect to the flower is represented by a dot on the top of the floral diagram. Calyx, corolla, androecium and gynoecium are drawn in successive whorls, calyx being the outermost and the gynoecium being in the centre. Floral formula also shows cohesion and adhesion within parts of whorls and between whorls. The floral diagram and floral formula shown in above figure represents the mustard plant (family; Brassicaceae).

Floral diagram:

- It is a diagrammatic representation of ground plane of a flower in bud condition as observed in transverse section with respect to mother axis, showing relationship of various floral parts of each type, their cohesion or adhesion, monothecous or bithecous nature of anthers, their dehiscence, placentation, nectaries, disc, etc. Various symbols used for drawing the floral diagram are shown below:

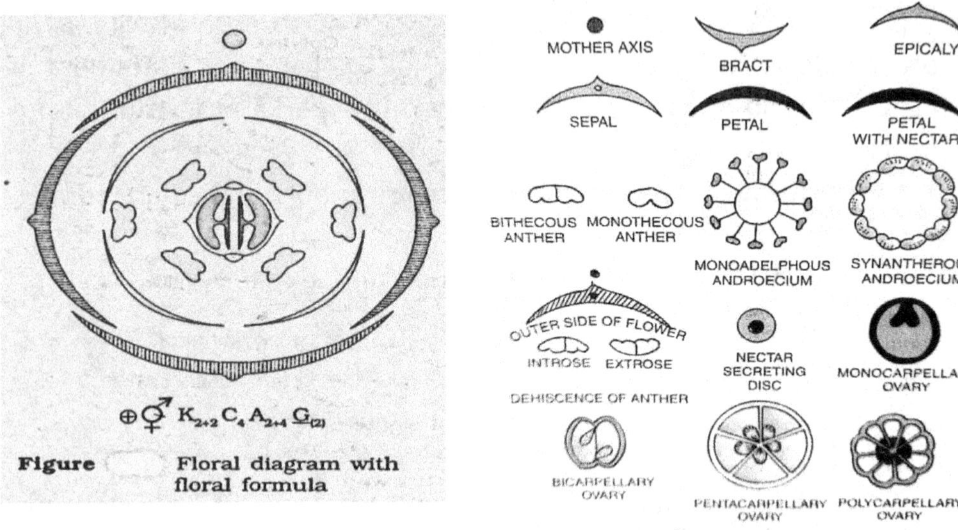

$\oplus \, \male\female \ K_{2+2} \, C_4 \, A_{2+4} \, \underline{G}_{(2)}$

Figure   Floral diagram with floral formula

Description of some important families

Fabaceae:

The family was earlier called papilionoideae, a subfamily of family leguminosae. It is distributed all over the world.

Vegetative characters

Trees, shrubs, herbs; root with root nodules

Stem: erect or climber

Leaves: alternate, pinnately compound or simple; leaf base, pulvinate; stipulate; venation reticulate.

Floral characters:

Inflorescence: raecmose

Flower: bisexual, zygomorphic

Calyx: sepals five, gamosepalous: imbricate aestivation

Corolla: petals five, polypetalous, papilionaceous, consisting of a posterior standard, two lateral wings, two anterior one forming a keel (enclosing stamens and pistil, vexillary aestivation.

Androecium: ten, diadelphous, anther dithecous

Gynoecium: ovary superior, mono carpellary, unilocular with many ovules, style single

Fruit: legume, seed: one to many, non – endospermic

Floral Formula: $\% \, \male \, K_{(5)} \, C_{1+2+(2)} \, A_{(9)+1} \, \underline{G}_1$

Many plants belonging to the family are sources of pulses (gram, arhar, moong, soyabean, edible oil (soyabean, groundnut); dye (indigofera); fibres (Sunhemp); fodder (Sesbania, trifolium), ornamentals (lupin, sweet pea); medicine (muliathi)

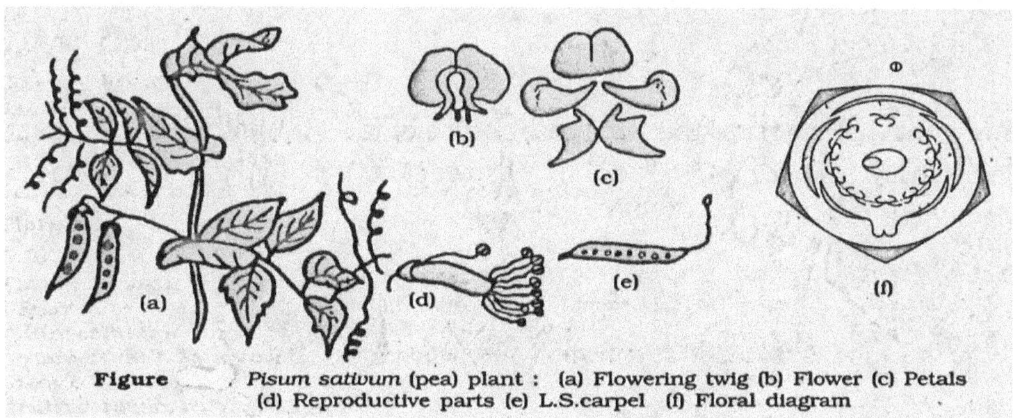

Figure . *Pisum sativum* (pea) plant : (a) Flowering twig (b) Flower (c) Petals (d) Reproductive parts (e) L.S.carpel (f) Floral diagram

Solanaceae:

It is a large family, commonly called as the 'potato family'. It is widely distributed in tropics, subtropics and even temperate zones.

Vegetative characters: plants mostly herbs, shrubs and rarely small trees.

Stem: herbaceous rarely woody, aerial, erect, cylindrical, branched, solid or hollow, hairy or glabrous, underground stem in potato (*Solanum tuberosum*)

Leaves: alternate, simple, rarely pinnately compound, exstipulate: venation reticulate

Floral characters:-

Inflorescence: solitary, axillary or cymose as in solanum

Flower: bisexual, actinomorphic

Calyx: sepals five, united: persistent valvate aestivation

Corolla: petals five: united: valvate aestivation

Androecium: stamens five, epipetalous

Gynoecium: bicarpellary, syncarpous: ovary: superior, bilocular, placenta swollen with many ovules

Fruits: berry or capsule

Seeds: many, endospermous

Floral formula: $\oplus \, \male\female \, K_{(5)} \, \overline{C_{(5)}} \, A_5 \, \underline{G}_{(2)}$

Economic importance:

Many plants belonging to the family are source of food (tomato, brinjal, potato), spice (chilli): medicine (belladonna, ashwagandha): fumigatory (tobacco): ornamentals (petunia)

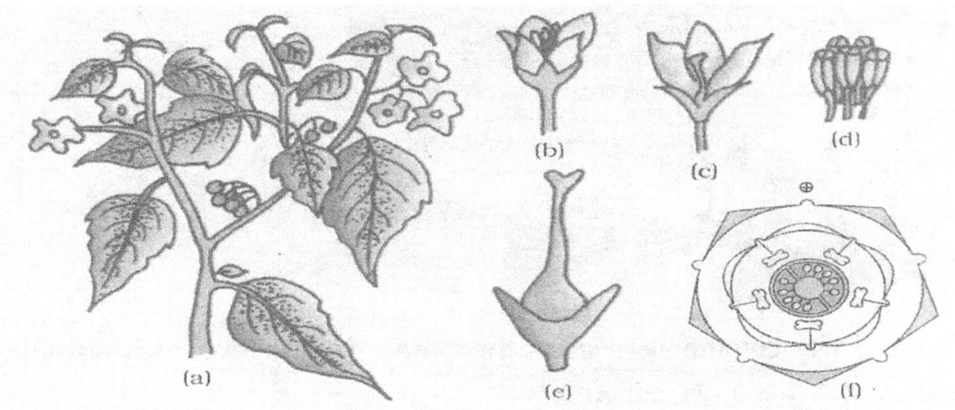

Figure *Solanum nigrum* (makoi) plant : (a) Flowering twig (b) Flower (c) L.S. of flower (d) Stamens (e) Carpel (f) Floral diagram

Liliaceae:

Commonly called the 'lily family' is a characteristic representative of monocotyledonous plants. It is distributed worldwide.

Vegetative characters: parental herbs with underground bulbs/corms/ rhizomes

Leaves mostly basal, alternate, linear, exstipulate with parallel venation

Floral characters

Inflorescence: solitary/ cymose; often umbellate clusters

Flower: bisexual; actinomorphic

Perianth tepal six (3+3), often united into tube: valvate aestivation

Androecium: stamen six,(3+3)

Gynoecium: tricarpellary, syncarous, ovary superior, trilocular with many ovules; axile placentation

Frit: capsule, rarely berry

Seed: endospermous

Floral formula: $\mathrm{Br} \;\oplus\; \male\female\; P_{3+3}\, A_{3+3}\; \underline{G}_{(3)}$

Economic importance: Many plants belonging to this family are good ornamentals (tulip, gloriosa), source of medicine (aloe), vegetables (asparagus), and colchicine (colchicum autumnale)

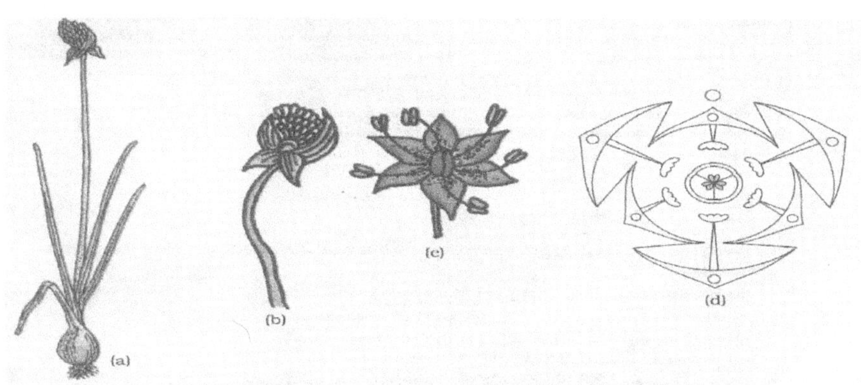

Figure   *Allium cepa* (onion) plant : (a) Plant (b) Inflorescence (c) Flower (d) Floral diagram

www.ingramcontent.com/pod-product-compliance
Lightning Source LLC
Chambersburg PA
CBHW081408130726
47998CB00011B/3110